AUTHENTIC CHINESE CUT-PAPER DESIGNS

Edited and Arranged
by

CAROL
BELANGER
GRAFTON

Dover Publications, Inc.
New York

Copyright © 1988 by Dover Publications, Inc.
All rights reserved under Pan American and International Copyright Conventions.

Published in Canada by General Publishing Company, Ltd., 30 Lesmill Road, Don Mills, Toronto, Ontario.

Authentic Chinese Cut-Paper Designs is a new work, first published by Dover Publications, Inc., in 1988.

DOVER *Pictorial Archive* SERIES

Manufactured in the United States of America
Dover Publications, Inc., 31 East 2nd Street, Mineola, N.Y. 1150!

Library of Congress Cataloging-in-Publication Data

Authentic Chinese cut-paper designs / edited and arranged by Carol Belanger Grafton.
    p.   cm. — (Dover pictorial archive series)
    ISBN 0-486-25775-4 (pbk.)
    1. Paper work—China—Themes, motives. 2. Decoupage—China—Themes, motives. I. Grafton, Carol Belanger. II. Series.
NK8553.2.C6A94 1988
736'.98'0951—dc19   88-16202
                         CIP

Publisher's Note

Cut-paper designs have long been recognized as one of the most outstanding of the Chinese folk arts. It was, of course, in China that paper was invented (by at least 100 A.D.), and it was there that paper crafts were developed to an outstanding degree, the first evidence of cut-paper designs dating from the Tang dynasty (618–906).

Traditionally, cut-paper designs were made by artisans who attached a stencil to several sheets of tissue paper and cut out the designs using a variety of tools including scissors, gouges, punches, knives and needles. The paper was frequently brightly colored. The paper designs, often given as gifts, were used for purposes as diverse as lantern decorations or embroidery patterns.

Recently, the Chinese have directed fresh attention to the ancient craft, although approaching it in a more modern manner, as shown in the examples reproduced here. For the most part, the designs depict flowers, animals and landscapes. Some of the religious subjects found in the older designs are no longer in evidence, but other traditional themes, such as the Imperial dragon (page 18) and the monkey king (page 19), serve as a link with the past.

40

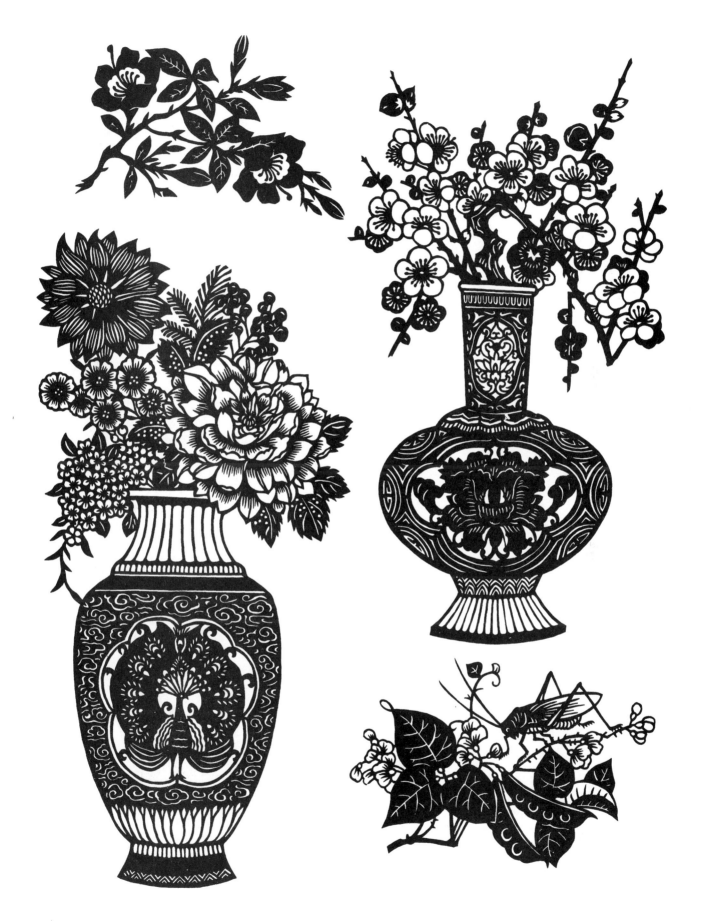

43